Running Away

poems by

Rebecca Guess Cantor

Finishing Line Press
Georgetown, Kentucky

Running Away

ACKNOWLEDGMENTS

Mezzo Cammin: "Girl" and "Second Date"
The Cresset: "The Day My Mother Died"

I am grateful to my husband, Ryan, who vowed on our wedding day
eleven years ago to always appreciate my shaped syllabics and has never
disappointed. I love this life we've woven together.

And I am grateful to my teachers, especially Kim Bridgford, who showed me
how to be a poet.

Editor: Christen Kincaid

Cover Art: Leanne Sargeant, leannesargeant.com

Author Photo: Ryan Cantor

Cover Design: Elizabeth Maines

Printed in the USA on acid-free paper.
Order online: www.finishinglinepress.com
also available on amazon.com

Author inquiries and mail orders:
Finishing Line Press
P. O. Box 1626
Georgetown, Kentucky 40324
U. S. A.

Table of Contents

For Carolyn, Cassie, Angela, and Norah

Running Away

I packed rice, soup,
an apple and I swore
that I would never
come back, not ever.
Mom *looked* sad at least.
*I hope you change your
mind*, she said, but she
let me go, and I
set out wearing my
almost empty back-
pack. I didn't know
what she was aiming
at, so helpful, so
complying. *Tie your
shoes*, she said, but I
didn't. I just left,
needing no one.
At the end of the block
I sat on the sidewalk
eating the apple
that was the color
of rust and spring
leaves, reading Uncle
Ben's box, realizing
I needed water and
heat and, oh yes,
I'd nowhere to stay.
A trail of ants found

my apple core and
began their work.
I told myself I should
go back, my sisters
needed me, and I
began the walk home.

A Good Day
Puget Sound, Washington

A good day was the day we decided
To keep going even when we'd reached
The state line, the hotel or motel
We'd planned to stop at, the break
In our long drive toward our grandparents'
House on green water, but because
We'd kept going we arrived at two or three
In the maroon-colored morning and didn't want
To wake them, startle them from sleep,
So we simply spread our blankets
On the dewy lawn and slept—five tired
But contented lumps in a row—
Until Grandpa in his age-worn robe,
Woke us and the sound with his laugh.

Camano Island
for William Symonds 1927-2015

I am one of five cousins sleeping
in a row of creaking cots, out
in Grandpa's shop. When I wake
I stumble
into the house, into the kitchen. My bare
toes find the cold floor and curl quickly.

Grandma's breakfast of bacon and eggs
stings the room, and the sun pouring
in through picture windows heats
my dark hair.
This is Camano Island, where we came each
weekend, where we now come each summer.

As children, we built driftwood ladders,
even though we'd nothing to climb.
In warm rain, we wore plastic
orange slickers
over t-shirts and underwear and bare feet.
The garish color clashed with gray sky.

Sun-stroked rocks warm the incoming tide,
but not enough. As kids we waited
for the sun to fade. The cool
evening dulled
the shock of frigid waves and uncles towed us
behind the boat. Our screams filled the sky.

There were never too many people,
but often there weren't enough beds.
We set up tents on the lawn,
and we slept
until the rain leaked through the thin, nylon roof,
when we ran inside, seeking shelter.

And then the rain stopped and years passed and
lightning began. As we stood on the
soggy lawn, we watched purple
streaks painting
a coal-colored sky. They dipped into the sound,
splashed, and lingered, printed behind my eyes.

When the woman was drowning, Grandpa
flew downstairs, rowed fiercely, started
the motor boat, and let the
dinghy drift
while he saved her sinking life. My cousins and
I had never seen the boat left untied.

My dad first came to Camano, came into
the family, when he was nineteen.
I brought my love this summer,
nineteen, too.
We drove up the 5, straight through California,
curving constantly through Oregon.

Finally, we crossed the Columbia
and we drove over the bridge that makes
the wooded island, and we
drove into
the arms of my past, his future, where lightning
still lingers firmly behind my eyes.

The Sound

My sister and I
step into our boats
and push off the shore,
letting bare toes drag
across the surface.
I dip an oar and pull.
I watch as its drops
pattern our section
of Puget Sound.
We drift and whisper,
drift and whisper
wanting to keep the
stillness of it to
ourselves, until the
water becomes black
against an orange-
red-gold-colored sky.

A seal, newly born,
startles us, kneads
at my boat. His eyes,
like black pearls, go
back and forth between
us as we whisper
warily to each
other and to him,
to each other, until
he leaves us alone
together on the water,
in the night, gone to
continue his search,

and we have nothing
to do but start in
toward land, leaving
behind the sound.

Aunt Sherry

I.

We're shopping, just her and me,
snaking through rows of racks.
She buys me an entire outfit—
backpack, skirt, jacket, shoes, shirt—
all made of denim and splashed
with pink. *No sisters on this trip*,
she says. *Just you and me.*
Great. Even my high top shoes
have flamingo laces that sparkle.

II.

She's here, we yell when she turns
into the driveway. *I'm here,* she echoes,
leaning halfway out her car window.
We hug, she kisses my forehead,
and we go to greet grownups inside.
And then she paints. Every room
is decorated with the paintings
and the houses she makes from driftwood
and nails and then adorns with a tiny brush:
shading awnings, creating door knobs,
curtains, window boxes full with flowers.
Bill's Biffy, she says, angling the facade
of a finished product toward me.
It's an outhouse. An outhouse!

III.

She isn't sick for long, but it's long
enough. Mom tells us Aunt Sherry
doesn't remember us anymore.
We send a Hallmark card with flowers
on the front that look bleak
compared to the ones she paints,
painted. Before my eyes they fade
and wilt turning a shade of brown
like wet sand packed under rocks.
We put our pictures in the card
so she'll remember us. *Remember me.*

IV.

I wear a velvet dress that itches my legs
and makes me feel guilty for feeling
pretty. In a basket by the door are
all the cards she's received in the past
week. And there's ours, still sealed.

I cry freely during the service.
I was afraid that the tears wouldn't come,
that I'd have to focus on the sting
in my eyes. Grandma laughs at my uncle's
jokes. We're only supposed to laugh quietly,
politely, and certainly through tears.

V.

While the adults sip and hug and cry,
my cousins and I play tag out back through
a garden of gladiolas and other church-like
flowers—through a maze of headstones
that remind me of boulders. We laugh
and scream and I run hard, each breath
coming from deeper than the one before.
My dress clings to my legs, my tears
dry to my cheeks, and I've been drained
until I'm full again, wishing that I was
wearing high tops instead of patent leather.

Couplets at Tea
for Peggy

We order flavors like mango and hibiscus,
Exotic flavors, tastes we've not yet tried,

Then spoon in sugars, pour in milk,
Watching them swirl around and down

Into our teas as the fifty years between us
Vanish like the steam. *We're an odd pair,*

You and I, she says. I laugh. It's true.
I look around at other friends better suited

And I shrug. I love the tiers of sandwiches
Cut into triangles, the scones and desserts

Dressing our mismatched plates, spread
Across the table like a quilt. We don't like tea,

But we go to read our poems: sonnets
And villanelles, couplets. My words flow

From the pages—she cries just a little,
And she's embarrassed. *You're too young*

To feel this deeply, she says between
The stanzas and I have nothing to say

To this woman who's lived so much life,
Who has felt so much more deeply than me,

I have nothing but my tea and the room
And her. And it's more than enough.

Girl

The rain falls coldly.
I see a girl and
The casual games she craves.
She runs past, hair spilling behind her.

I see a girl and
Her layered skirt, damp.
She runs past, hair spilling behind her,
Pink cheeks, pink purse, pink.

Her layered skirt damp
As she ignores the cold and wet, her
Pink cheeks, pink purse, pink
Lips she uses to kiss.

As she ignores the cold and wet, her
Charms cause boys to follow those
Lips she uses to kiss.
The boys hope that she is easy.

Charms cause boys to follow those
Girls who smile through the gray rain.
The boys hope that she is easy.
They see just a girl. They like

Girls who smile through the gray rain
And so they flirt and touch.
They see just a girl. They like
That they might have her,

And so they flirt and touch
As much as she will let them touch
That they might have her.
Until they pass her on.

As much as she will let them touch
She always thinks it's up to her
Until they pass her on.
And then she knows.

She always thinks it's up to her
The casual games she craves.
And then she knows—
The rain falls coldly.

The Song

I stood before you, a crowd of creaking,
And I was aware of my wearing not enough.
A man, his tongue resting on his lower lip,
Blew into the mic, smiled, and handing it to me,
Touched my arm as if to say, *Let's see.*
And you saw the words play before your eyes
And cheered at the high note—supported
My struggling-through, my curving ways—
Never understanding my words. And in the end
My beat continued. The man (who heard nothing)
Took back what was his, like it was an insult
In his hand. The song and I were done and
Even then, as I stood beneath the lights,
I knew that I would stand before you again.

Waiting in a Manhattan Lobby

In the swirl
and spill of carpet
she sees radii and line
split, splintered
before her until
purple-growing hyacinth
surround the moon
and she worries
that her orb of ghosts
and daily dreams
will be drowned by petals
as thin as rice paper,
as sheets of water on ice,
drops of almost ice.
And—six o'clock—
she feels smothered
by the weight
of a surrounding lobby,
another conversation
filled with meaning
nothing. And—
six o'three—she is
strangled by a lingering
gaze, by the smell
of perfume, by
the impulse to smile.

Second Date

We drive down Grove Street on our second date,
And though we're quiet the space is filled with shy
But daring looks. The car reflects the sky
As we breeze past, surrounded by the weight
Of storms that seem to hang above a great
Expanse of clouds. But one cloud doesn't try
To wait. It bursts alone and falls to dry
Pavement below. Instead of rushing by, my date
Just turns into a lot to chase the patch
Of rain that swirls around the trees, around
The cars, and trucks, the lamps and straight, white lines,
And we are brought together by the catch.
Then it's gone. We listen to the sound
Of breaths, of lives, that weave like climbing vines.

Diving In

We have a place in the park next to the lake,
under a tree. The grass is well watered
and soft, but we bring a blanket, a quilt
much too heavy for summer, and we lie
together watching, like in a movie montage.
We notice a bird circling over the lake.
He plunges into the water and we wait.
We hold our breath and each other and think
he'll never surface again. But he does,
his beak and feathers full of water, not fish.
He goes on circling. He circles the green
and sun and taste of it all and plunges.
I look back at this man I have been circling
for months. And I am ready to dive in.

In the Rain

It's raining so hard that the drops jump off
the pavement. Trees bend. Rain buries itself
in your sweater. You realize it's no help,
but you trudge on until he's there, buying
his coffee from a vendor on the street. He must
have been running late today for your paths
to cross. The rain can't get through his coat,
but his hair is matted to his face, the face
you know so well, the face you will sleep
beside tonight. And he laughs with you
at your sorry state and you laugh at his and
you kiss. You're as warm as you were minutes
before the alarm, and you know he's the only
one who could warm you here, in the rain.

Sleep Walking

In the blackness of two a.m.
she felt him leave her
side. Still sleeping
he took the blankets,
slid them from her
naked body and lay down
on the hardwood floor,
somehow more content.

He had always liked to move
in his sleep, needing to drift,
to find a new place.
In those moments
she loved him like a child.

She crawled until
she found him—
his outstretched arm.
Pillowing herself,
she kissed his slightly
open mouth and joined him
in his wandering sleep.

Aubade

He sings—
not well but sweet
like plums as weather
warms bare skin,
bare skin,
bare skin.

The God-sky
pours like sugar
over young girls,
blue skirts that spin
with pale dancing legs.

As long
as we hold our breath
the hummingbird
is still.

Inside lunaria
like paper lanterns
light our room,
our sonnet square
and full until—

Aubade—
we welcome
the morning
by staying in bed.

Morning

The morning stings me
from the first. Sifting through
the dark, water left running,
a too-bright lamp, a tangled
slip, cat staring, ignored.
He snores. I brush through
tangled morning hair,
pull three gray ones—
wonder how long
my mom's been dyeing.

I stand at my closet,
trying to remember the last time
I did laundry, the last time
I felt comfortable in my skin.
And he snores as the cat paws
at his nose, expecting more
luck with him than me.
I overflow her bowl just to show her.

Outside the day is clear and blue
and smells like pine
or fabric softener. I stop—
frozen in the early sun, angry
at the discordant scene,
at the simple, at the beautiful—
just angry. Keys in my hand,
I melt beneath the weight.

Tulips

She's leaning downward
on all fours—her gloved hands
in the dirt, clawing for the three
inches needed for tulip bulbs—
when he sees her, likes what he sees,
and crosses the cul-de-sac.

Looks like rough work, he says,
standing above her in the sun.
She squints uncomfortably
but smiles just the same.
She says something about
it being worth it in the spring.

He doesn't answer, just stands
above her looking down
her top, stained with dirt, stained
with clover and dirt. She sits
back and adjusts her straps.
Looks good, he says, and goes.

The Day My Mother Died

The day my mother died
I went to the grocery store
And bought grapes and tea
And pasta. My sister called.
We talked about the reunion
And made a date for coffee
Early Wednesday morning.

The day my mother died
I went to the post office
To mail her birthday present.
It cost eight dollars to mail
The brown paper package
Which hid a patchwork quilt.
My daughter drew a snowflake
On the wrapping even though
My mother died in July.

The day my mother died
I picked my son up from school.
He was assigned a family tree
For homework. While I cooked
In the kitchen, I dictated dates—
Births and deaths and marriages.
My daughter drew a blue daffodil
That I was hanging on the fridge
When my sister called again
And told me my mother had died.

12 Trees

In the SoCal suburb
where we lived for four years
in a hundred-year-old house
with a bedroom and a half,
with a fruit cellar,
the trees were always in bloom—
a different tree, it seemed,
every month. So I had an idea

to plant 12 trees in our front yard,
12 trees in a long row,
in the order that they would bloom,
and I would look out the window
while doing the dishes or look up
from my writing, and I would say,
juniper, it must be April,
and I would say, magnolia,
it must be May. Of course,

Bank of America took that house
(do not, if you can avoid it,
buy anything in 2007)
before we could even dig the holes.
We planted an avocado tree,
to be sure, but no crabapple.
No cassia tree. And yet, even today,
our credit quite recovered,
I can still see the trees blooming
in their row, and I think,
floss silk tree, it must be October.

Having Room

The family room was small for so many children,
For so many years. There was always someone

Left on the floor, always someone fighting
For the splitting leather of my husband's chair.

They were all I'd ever wanted—children, a family.
But now I'm left in this room that grows

As my children leave me with a man I once knew.
I cleaned in circles, always picking up a room,

Another, a third, then circling back to the first.
Now empty rooms stay clean. I'm blanketed

In photos framed in silver—their cheeks
Pressed against the glass, memories in their eyes

That look like mine. My husband's chair is cold
And rough against my face. Soon he'll be home,

And he'll ask how my day was. I'll ask how his
Was instead, and he'll ask if I've heard from the kids.

The Photographer

You used to take photographs.
You used to shoot leaves and shoes
and fountains. You loved light—
the way it changed things,

like seeing through Monet's eyes.
You loved the way the morning's sun
could paint a building, reflecting
off stone like physics. A force

in your life, it compelled you to snap
pictures of roofs and faces and him.
You thought that you had to take
those pictures—bottles and bridges,

a cross—just like great writers say:
I was meant to write. But a picture
is not what you want, when the wind
turns and he leaves you with moments

and exits caught on film, broken glass,
broken bones, broken will. No.
You've stopped taking pictures
of this life you would rather forget.

Crosswalk

She waits at the edge of a crosswalk
For a faceless man to tell her it's safe
To cross the blurred stream of traffic

While air as warm as breath rushes
In the open windows of passing cars.

A taste of cologne is caught by a current
Of wind and reaches toward her.

Quietly, she says hello to her remembered husband.

Forty, fifty years ago, when things
Moved slower, or she was faster,
They would always take their time.

She made him laugh, her red-haired husband,
The way no one else ever could when she stirred

More than circles of dust in a crosswalk.

The man signals to her, and she steps out
Into the street—ten degrees warmer—
And the crosswalk sighs beneath her,

Bored by her pace. Halfway across she's hurried
By a red-flashing hand and she briefly
Quickens her step. But instead, she stops.

Laughing, she faces the sky with her arms
Spread wide and turns in a circle once,

Twice: finally remembering her husband
And not just that he's gone. The light

Turns green, and she smiles at the cars,
At her husband, to herself, and she moves on,

Following the crosswalk and taking her time.

Rebecca Guess Cantor received her Ph.D. in American Literature from Claremont Graduate University, her Master's in English and Creative Writing from Loyola Marymount University, and her B.A. in English and Religious Studies at Fairfield University in Connecticut where she also played division I volleyball. A native Washingtonian, Rebecca enjoys visiting her family up north in the summer, dinners out with her husband, reading Dr. Seuss to John and Norah, singing, board games, and museums. She is currently the Assistant Provost at Azusa Pacific University where she has also served as the Executive Director of Writing Programs and teaches writing and literature from time to time. She takes after her father, Del. Rebecca's poetry has appeared in *Mezzo Cammin*, *Two Words For*, *The Cresset*, *The Lyric*, and *Silver Birch Press*, among other publications.

www.ingramcontent.com/pod-product-compliance
Lightning Source LLC
LaVergne TN
LVHW091235080426
835509LV00009B/1291